The Paper Girl

poems by

Jessica M. Brophy

Finishing Line Press
Georgetown, Kentucky

The Paper Girl

Copyright © 2016 by Jessica M. Brophy
ISBN 978-1-63534-002-0 First Edition
All rights reserved under International and Pan-American Copyright Conventions. No part of this book may be reproduced in any manner whatsoever without written permission from the publisher, except in the case of brief quotations embodied in critical articles and reviews.

ACKNOWLEDGMENTS

A very special thanks goes to my first poetry-mother, Dr. Monifa Love Asante, who believed in my voice and called me daughter. I am equally grateful to the other poet-warriors in my life—Laura Long, Marilyn Bousquin, Jen Coleman, and Jer Bryant—who helped support the birth of this chapbook.

Publisher: Leah Maines

Editor: Christen Kincaid

Cover Art: Daniel Brophy

Author Photo: Jessica M. Brophy

Cover Design: Jessica M. Brophy

Printed in the USA on acid-free paper.
Order online: www.finishinglinepress.com
        also available on amazon.com

Author inquiries and mail orders:
Finishing Line Press
P. O. Box 1626
Georgetown, Kentucky 40324
U. S. A.

Table of Contents

- Front Page News 1
- Doxology 3
- Altar Call 4
- Evening Prayer for Father 5
- A Dirty Miracle 6
- Tammy Salombine 7
- Magnolia Jungle 8
- Mrs. Hennessey 9
- Mrs. Messersmith 10
- The Bauer Family 11
- A Brick Row House of Retirees 12
- Back Scratches 13
- When Mom Was Angry 15
- Dad Gives Me Roses 18
- Hiding 19
- The Shipley's 20
- Martinez 21
- Male Boxing 22
- I Finger Myself 24
- Horror 25
- Sunday Afternoon Trilogy 26
- What I Learned About Sex from My Parents 29
- Down The Hill 30
- My First Piece of Real Jewelry 31

To my brothers and sisters—you inspire me.

FRONT PAGE NEWS

She is proud of her feat, worthy
of front page news
alongside headlines about Paris bombings,
the FBI violating students' rights,
Jackie O in a two-piece evening gown,
and a recipe for tuna-ghetti.

Mom is looking at my twin brother
with her twenty-nine year old glow.
We are famous for a day.
Mom is adoring Matt
who rests on her right shoulder,
flares his nostrils out,
puckers his lips like he's waiting for a kiss.
I am sleeping calmly, sprawled out on her left shoulder
half of my face covered in blanket.

The cop who delivered me at home
stands beaming behind Mom.
He tells the reporter: "You just have to pull
them out a little bit, but it was easy."

I am the daughter of a woman
who made the news
for bringing me to life
while making it look easy.

I am a child pulled by a cop,
with the help of our neighbors
and my older siblings.
I am the younger twin,
a body still comfortable
with 6 o'clock entries into the light.

I am a newborn of a town hero,
a side-kick to a boy.

Already doing his rounds
at the Rickles warehouse,
I am the daughter of a man
who missed my arrival.

DOXOLOGY

We rise in unison
to the faith's doxology—
rag dolls with strings
sewn in the back of our necks.
We are marionettes,
our heads bobbling
shoulders shrugging
joint to ear, joint to ear.

The militancy in the rhythm of the hymn
mixed with the march of the ushers
down the center aisle, the velvet plates
levitating saucers before their
erect bodies and one swinging arm,
is somehow a welcomed release.

Repeating "Praise Him"
is all we have left
to give—two small
words thanking him
for not being paralyzed,
thanking him because in
the moment we rise
we can wish
to be transported
back to a playful stage
where the puppeteers
were the Von Trapp children
and the puppets yodeled,
drank beer,
and had goats as friends.

ALTAR CALL

I slide forward and rest my head on the oak pew in front of me.
I feel delight in that moment between the last word of the sermon and the altar invitation.
I feel content at this temporary break to fall over and enjoy sleep during service.

But I like to watch the altar too—

> Joe Matloz cradles his industrial set of keys when he kneels. He supports his elbows on the altar step and clasps his hands so they touch his nose. There is peace in his palms. His hair swoop smells like spiced gel.
>
> Roy Baranyay flanks the right side. He prays like an angel—soft grey flannel pants, white button down, no tie, saltine cracker eye spectacles.
>
> Jim Costello bends his knees slowly, placing his hands out to catch his collapse.
>
> Pastor Frank perches from above on stage. His body sits erect on the padded chair. His crossed leg swings to a military cadence. He stretches his neck back and imagines his time in Vietnam—a shirtless, skinny Sicilian killing in the jungle.

I sit back and doze during the final amen, then open my eyes.
Turning away from the altar to face the week.
Trying to imagine my own prayers.

EVENING PRAYER FOR FATHER

Where did he learn to love?
Did he have a father?
Did his mother rub his back in church,
cook his favorite meal before he went away,
brag about him to the Peruvian neighbors,
Roger and Violeta,
sign him up for craft Thursdays?

His mother brags that she fed him sandy
bologna sandwiches on the Jersey Shore.

*Not once did my mother tell me
she loved me*, dad says.
She did stack the presents high
on Christmas morning,
letting the twelve children
each keep one and
returning the rest to Woolworth's.

Tonight he proudly retells the
the violent nights, the dangerous
days of living with his father and brothers.
Mother was a target too
of her husband's knuckles.

When do our crutches
give us dignity?
It isn't absurd for him to
hold his head high?
It isn't vainglory
to keep it inside,
exhaling it
on special occasions?

Isn't having a story better
than none at all?

A DIRTY MIRACLE

Chicken roll has a grainy flap.
It rides the middle plane between royalty and common wealth.
The miracle whirl whips over the grit and tastes
   like sea-battered goodness.
Chicken roll is a delicacy for kids on peanut butter and pasta diets.
The mealy-round slices satisfy the craving for a wild substance,
for a gritty wholeness,
for a complete father who doesn't feel self-conscious
about buying his children
second-class chicken
with its speckled bits
of beige anonymity.

TAMMY SALOMBINE

In exchange for a perfectly arranged French braid
grafted like an antiqued rose on a cobwebbed branch,
Tammy Salombine would agree to fold the bundles of papers
dropped underneath our Norway Maple.

Some days news was light,
like when Michael won a Grammy for Moonwalker
or the Rubik's Cube was invented.
On these days, Tammy stacked each paper
so that together they looked like
an upside-down sugar cone.

Other times, news was heavy.
Exxon was spilling oil in the Valdez,
Oliver North was taking the fifth amendment,
and Ryan White was dying.
Her perfectly folded stack looked like the Pyramids.

Tammy was in a mentally-handicapped class at our church,
probably the happiest member,
a person who was never ashamed of saying *I love you*.
When the bundles arrived late, she'd place them straight
into my older siblings' canvas slings
with their thick orange straps.

Tammy knew how to make a fair deal
to gather her thick brown-blond hair
into a 'do my mother ensured
would last a whole week.
It hurt a little.

MAGNOLIA JUNGLE

A detour off the sidewalk
into a magnolia tree jungle
right between Milton and Maple Avenues
on someone else's property
is the escape I need
before returning home from school.
The glistening fat leaves,
the scent of lemon verbena
from the flower bulbs,
the canopy of dense shade,
hide me from the dangers of reason,
reality, the rut of a child's work routine
and let me feel a dirt floor, soft windows,
a hidden entrance and exit.
The jungle lets me look out on my path,
peep through the lines of sun
and dodge pinecones and needles
like a running back.

MRS. HENNESSEY: 337 WEST MILTON

Mom has rubber-banded my stack
already waiting on the front porch,
with baby Ben in his play pen.
A paper girl in training.

The foyer where I wait to be buzzed in
doesn't mix well with the smell of newspaper ink on my fingertips.
The ink's warm pungency and band's vinegar bite
collide with cheap carpet and microwaved food being prepared inside.
You let me in after you ask, "Who is it?" and I sing, "Pay-purr Gurrrl."

Seniors at the Clifford Case Apartments sit relaxed in the lobby,
their bums enjoying the boxed chairs you'd find
next to a college dormitory's vending machine.

I knock on your door. You answer it, using the help of your walker.
Like every day before, I wait to be rewarded with
    two Twizzler cherry sticks.
You ask me today, *What happened to your face? It looks like*
    you got into a fight.
Did someone punch you?

I am 10 or 11.
I don't have the language
or awareness to tell you
that my face was born with these marks—
a port-wine birthmark, or a stain if you like.
Instead, my body reacts to your nosy questions.
My throat swells up and my eyes fill with warm tears.

Do I look injured?
Strangers pity me?
I leave not knowing how
to narrate what others see.

MRS. MESSERSMITH: 415 ELM AVE.

You project an image of a wife with a stately home, winning daughters, and enough money to keep it cool through retirement. You had the longest path to the front door my bike had to travel, your lawn covered with ivy.

I know the smell of your home because you always invite me into your foyer while you dig out the $2.60 for one week's paper subscription. Your home smells rich: some mix of wild cherry bing, imitation vanilla, butter, and lemon Pledge—undeniable assurance that life was okay. Suits in dry-cleaning plastic schlump near the carpeted stairwell, resting on Italian walnut chairs, their sexy backs and legs spread open, the cushion seats raised and ready to swallow somebody's bottom.

I never saw your husband. You ran a lot of errands for him. And from the looks of your entryway, couldn't keep up with the clutter left over from Lord and Taylor bags, receipts, and unused bowties bought while you were shopping alone.

THE BAUER FAMILY: 418 ELM AVE.

One glorious afternoon, you invite me and Mary over for popcorn and chocolate milk, Campbell's tomato soup, and *Annie*.

We lounge in the finished basement, girls who have their own space to play. In this household, sisters are treated like Anastasias, each daughter possessing her own bedroom, her own dreams, her own voice to talk with her mustached-commuting father.

Each daughter expected to make something of herself—to attend Rutgers or Fairleigh Dickinson. To marry for love and tradition. To defer to father's advice and engage in mother's stained glass hobbies.

While we lived on the same block of firmament, I can't help but feeling that I was just their paper girl, that we were a family of paper deliverers who didn't just need the route to be taught responsibility, but needed it to buy milk, bread, cheese, and butter.

Campbell's was out of the question.

A BRICK ROW HOUSE OF RETIREES

You sat on your porch like it was your living room.
The mistress wearing her house dress and curlers.
The master wearing a button-down pajama top and soft slippers.

Landscaping your small plot of lawn with tropical fauna,
plastic pink flamingos, overgrown shrubbery,
and an ankle-length plastic border fence,
you had decided to transport your retired Floridian lives
and put them on display in the front yard.

You were chain smokers and sat hunched over in your lawn chairs,
eating TV dinners on snack trays, the ash from your cigs floating
and resting on the tips of the Astroturf rug.

BACK SCRATCHES

Lying on her stomach with such longing,
mother would call for us to appear at her bedside
offering a dollar or sometimes five
if she was really itchy.
Her back was plump spotted
with soft brown moles
her shirt around her neck—
a little embarrassed—*don't look
at my small boobs.*

She'd grunt if we stopped,
tell us where to scratch the hardest—
lower back, the sides, the wings, down the spine—
Our hands would get tired
and she'd say *don't stop.*

We were only girls,
Mary and I, with our barter system.
We'd exchange a back rub for a back rub.
I'll do you if you'll do me,
pulling our shirts over our heads
dictating what we needed.

A little down.
No, to the right.
Little more.
Right above the butt cheek.
Yes. good. Urrrrrr.

We wanted a scratch too
so we'd request the scratch
be saved for the final minute
but smoothed over with the
massaging hands one last time.
If you received a rub last,
you could slip into the dreamworld
like a rubber on cock
or a peel opening.
This was the desired rhythm.
Giving first.
Receiving last.

WHEN MOM WAS ANGRY

1.
She'd tell us to hold our ankles
while she beat us with a freshly cut
dowel from the hardware store—she
got 'em made special—
the green or yellow chalk mark
on the end of the stick smudging
the bed sheet. Our heads
popping up and down in rhythm
with the strike of the stick on our unpadded arses,
wanting so badly to lay palms
on the bedsheets
or just take the beating standing up.
At least we could squeeze our butt between
blows to soften the anger.

Mom! I'm sorry. Please stop.

She boasted to other parents
about the gift she brought back
from Lancaster—
a glazed wooden paddle
with brown tree knots decorating its surface
an illustration of a cottage and a smoking
chimney on the fat end,
a red suede tie fastened on the skinny
end to hang on display.

Mom was angry often enough, and this is when
she spanked us. Cursing our father for
not doing it himself, she took out her frustration
on us. If she couldn't make him a good Baptist or
a carpenter, she would let us know this is what
she wanted in a man.

2.
Her wooden Dr. Scholl flip flops
served as anus intimidator
in the aisles of A and P.
Her right foot kicking us in our crack
knocking the air out of us
leaving us bent over
on the floor
in the shadow of her bulk.

Leaving us wondering if we were
as bad as she said we were.
One of us plotting how to hide
the spoon, the stick, the paddle, the belt
so she wouldn't have what she needed
in the heat of her uprising.

Out of the eight of us,
I don't know which one of us
hid the sticks. Mom did always
say Matt got the most beatings:
He should be proud of that.

3.
It was supposed to be a defense of marriage.
Dr. James Dobson titled his book *Dare to Discipline,*
a right wing ideology for corporeal punishment
keeping couples from divorcing one another
since they could focus so much time on punishing their children.

The doctor says the "shoulder muscle [when pinched] is ideal
for causing the maximum amount of pain."

Even when you are in public, if you get a Dobson pinch
the pain is not so obvious to shoppers
passing by in their grocery carts.

Because you aren't screaming.
Your face scrunches up.
and the mouth makes an O shape.
The neck kinks
and the knees cave.
You are in hero's pose with your head bowed
in between the sugar puffs and granola.

DAD GIVES ME ROSES

I got my period in the adult section of the library. It comes as brown mucus streaked with a wide paint brush in my underwear. I cry when I walk home. I don't know why I am crying. I just know something is wrong. I know my mother will treat me differently. I was in seventh grade loving Mrs. Dillemuth's home economics class, having just been introduced to recipes, Miss Piggy's Punch, and how to make English scones. This would change too. It was on a Saturday. My dad bought me red roses. It's the only time I remember him buying me flowers. I suspect the flowers were mother's idea. Mary is not around. I need her. She is younger than me by eighteen months, but in all things womanly, she is my muse. She has already practiced playing with boys.

HIDING

My mother never wears slacks. She is forever that girl mortified when her mother asks the sales lady, *Where is the Little Miss Chubbette section?* Mom wears long skirts over a belly, eight times a child bearer. Even though she hasn't gotten pregnant since 1986, as far as she's told me, she still carries a belly. The waists of her skirts always ride atop her belly. She hates to wear belts. She is hiding under those skirts, sometimes rubbing her belly when she has eaten a whole bag of chocolates. There is one skirt in particular that I remember well—a jean skirt. It went to her ankles, was a light wash, had a zipper down the front of the crotch, and a kangaroo pouch in the front with two large pockets. This was an all-purpose wardrobe item. She went shopping in it, cleaned in it, met other moms in it, went to church in it, and comforted my brother in it after he broke his ankle. It was a skirt you could consider a member of the family—an honorary Brophy. I don't know for sure, but I bet we tugged on that long skirt, looked under it, dirtied it with mustard and ketchup, and wondered what was underneath it— that parachute of denim. As long as I wore one, I could go roller skating with the church group.

THE SHIPLEY'S: 675 ELM ST.

I walk past your house
on my way to middle school.
Sometimes, you'll ask me
if I'd like a ride.
If I'm early, you offer me a bagel with lox,
the news on in the den,
the wood floors shiny.

You are both academics
who wear penny loafers and
button down collared shirts
with the top button unbuttoned,
live in a colonial style home
with a ramp to accommodate
grandmothers.
You have two children,
Sam and Laura, both
who have obvious
and controlled bounces in their steps.

You embody all that is good
about the WASP:
proudly calling grandma Queenie,
teaching middle school math and
high school English in town,
showing me the life of an academic
can be modest, disciplined, and caring.

MARTINEZ: 1242 BRYANT ST.

You live alone
and keep to yourself,
and even if you are in
a long-term relationship,
the neighbors
wouldn't know it.
You are Martinez.
Not the Martinezes.
And not like Madonna.
or Prince.
or Boy George.
We call you
by your last name—
as if it were your
first name.
As if you had
earned the respect
of just being called
by your last name.
A Cadillac in the driveway,
a family
of one.
A little defiant
in your independence,
the fluffy hair
and frosty lipstick
a ruse
to being so
exposed
on the corner lot
in a one-level
white house
with no fence
to keep intruders out.

MALE BOXING

The mother and daughters pushed with all
their might to keep father
down in the basement
booby trapped
with sump pumps,
leaky foundations,
gaping holes leading to
neglect and sewage.

We locked him out of the house
the back door
the front door
the door that
led down to
the basement
because he thought
his son was someone he
wanted to brawl.

Father wanted to crush him under
the weight of insult
to beat him with a belt
till he had won,
wanted to strangle Matt's beautiful
teenage body till the foam
from his mouth dripping
onto his son's face
told him
he had become
the old man
hitting his children.
This is conjecture,
but the father leaves
his daughters no choice

but to discover details
about his boyhood
out of their own
fiery imaginations
and from the scraps
of his memory that
leave us holding pieces.

I FINGER MYSELF

I explored my vagina when Mary slept over at her friend's house. I would hump pillows, stick my hips into the air while my chest remained on the bed, and construct imaginative patterns to vary the choreography of masturbation—circling, squaring, spiraling, unlatching. Our mattress laid on top of a metal box spring, so I could hear these patterns out loud and tried to mute them as best I could, although I secretly enjoyed how my body could direct a choir of squeaky, bouncy, panting notes. My parent's bedroom was just one story below and I never heard any sounds reaching me and Mary. When they divorced, the box spring had to be cut in half with a chainsaw just to get it down the stairs and onto the curb.

HORROR

We are sitting on a long 1970s couch that is paisley, polyester, and beige. The carpet is maroon. Six seventeen-year-old women from New Jersey line up, posing for a picture from a wide angle. One of the mothers must be taking the picture, capturing her daughter as a senior in high school with her girlfriends.

We may have been heading out for a night of mini-golf. Maybe we were going to the movies. Perhaps we were just making a night out of Italian ice or Mexican food.

Based on our postures, the occasion seems important. We pose like debutantes, housewives, or pageant contestants. Tara, Kelly, Cindy, April, Chrissy—our legs pointing in the same direction, our shoulders slightly turned in, our smiles carefree but involuntary.

I look like a vampire in the photo. Trying to cover my birthmark, I've used too much white powder again. My lips are walnut purple, and I have red eyes. I look scary among the other girls with tanned faces, straight hair, and athletic arms. I look half dead.

I am horrified. What was I trying to do, erase my face? Pretend I look more normal without the birthmark? That I could ingratiate them with an appearance they found familiar? That if I annihilated what I hated about myself they would love me?

SUNDAY AFTERNOON TRILOGY

1.
The shotgun skidding the pinna of the groom's ear at the altar,
put a few chinks in the couple's wedding day.
Thirteen days before their second anniversary,
the woman's womb had two more dents in it.

With the arrival of twins, number four and number five,
in 1979, the lady found Jesus Christ, superstar,
and a slit formed in their sheets.
It was narrow but long.

Holes began to widen in the linens till they gaped.
By baby number eight, the mother had left the home
and broke into the real world.

Standing on one side of the canyon, the father on the other,
there were no rules still pressuring them to stay
married, no religion keeping
the man undecided, and no more children
to want to ignore the chasm.

2.
We knew our parent's marriage was broke on Sundays.
After a decade of church compliance,
Dad began to shop for groceries instead
on Sunday mornings.

He formed a friendship with the woman
who fried the chicken in the prepared food section
at Pathmark.
She was a short black woman
who wore a white lab coat and
a fast food cap.

After Sunday dinner of fried chicken
and potato salad with egg,
this unspeakable thing happened.
We dispersed.

Dad could be found horizontal on the couch.
Mom was fixing lesson plans.
I and my siblings?
We did nothing on Sabbath afternoons
except worry about Monday coming.

No longer lulled by lunch's heaven
or put to slumber by the pastor's droning,
the Lord's Day lost its comfort.

We sensed it wasn't about us.
Mom wanted Dad to practice God like she did.

What remained was this gap of time on
Sunday afternoon filled with loss—
the loss of sleep when you need it,
the loss that staying quiet imposes,
the distance between our parent's gulf.

3.
A lapse,
something unaccounted for,
a temporary vacancy of control
on Sunday afternoons
puttied the fissure
from all those years
that fractured them.

For the children,
Church loses its consoling touch
Sunday its rest
The Lord some power.

They don't like to be quiet on
Sunday afternoons anymore
or nap too long
or stay too still
or consider why God
lost his touch.

They don't want to live
in the space between
mumbling groans
loud snores
and nothing to say.

WHAT I LEARNED ABOUT SEX FROM MY PARENTS

Mom went to wash her hands after
emerging from the bedroom,
the door never totally closed,
my dad never adept at
basic hardware fixes.

Wearing a light rose slip
and an over the shoulder, extra-large
t-shirt, Mom was comfortable.

Dad always remained behind,
sleeping into the next
work day.

It was on a Sunday.
The house was as quiet as
it'd ever be.

I never heard Mom squeal
or groan or say, *that
hurt*s. I never heard
anything from inside.

Just the door opening,
the faucet running,
mom combing her hair
back with a banana clip.

DOWN THE HILL

No one wanted to deliver to a route called Down the Hill,
a route at such a far corner of the beat
that we began to identify it by its long slope down
rather than our customer's last names.

Did we dread the strenuous bike ride back up hill?
Did we smell the chemicals from Hamilton Laundry
evaporating off the Rahway River?
Did we pretend the hill a slide to play on,
forgetting we were on the job?

Did St. Mary's nearby remind us of life before fundamentalism?
Did we crave the communal meals in the refectory?
Did our parent's marriage go down the hill the moment Dad left
the religion of his upbringing?

How many years had their
marriage been going down the hill?
Were they a sturdy brick exterior from the front side
but a flooding backyard the size of a football field
on the rotting back porch?

MY FIRST PIECE OF REAL JEWELRY

I am a heart. I am a heart that holds nothing. I can hold some things if you want to stuff me. I can be opened. I am real silver. I am stone grey now. Each half of me puffs out like the half of a chicken breast, its skin pulled back, waiting to be cut from the rest of its body on the carving board. An artist has cut swirls into my face. Stems without flowers. Leaves without buds. Wrinkles around the mouth without lips. A seamstress has done a zig-zag stitch around my edges.

Open me. I become two hearts. My edges are charred. My insides iridescent. Silver white light hits the corners of each eye. I am held together by a doll-house door hinge.

I am one charm on a cheap necklace. The other charms holds a picture frame of Frida Kahlo. She stares at me. In the picture frame, she wears beaded chandelier earrings, her hair is held up by two symmetrical buns with red ribbons round the bands. Her face is a close up. She is daring me to hold the artist inside. Her ears are stern, her jaw correct.

The edges of the pancakes on the stove are burning; the pot-holed half of the pancake is dry now. I will flip them, return to the stove. Recover what I can.

Jessica Margaret Brophy is a New Jersey native and a poet who writes about family quirks, nature's luster, childhood foods, the body, and spiritual identity. She is also a scholar of the sublime, addressing issues within women's studies and the black aesthetic of African American female poets. She has published scholarship on the poetry of Sharon Olds, Jean Toomer, Paulette Childress White, and Rita Dove. She teaches as a freelance academic at both Lynchburg College and the local community college. Among other journals, her poetry has appeared in *Natural Bridge: A Journal of Contemporary Poetry*, *Alimentum: The Literature of Food*, and *Awakenings Review* and is forthcoming in a special poetry anthology of *Blue Lyra Review*, Parts of the Whole: Poetry of the Body.

Only until she began writing about the port wine stain birthmark on her face (about three years ago) was she able to find a language to write about anything else. She knew her first collection of poetry would have to be about who she was before finding this language—the observing, questioning, reflecting child. Brophy is currently the creative writing editor at The First Unitarian Church of Lynchburg, Virginia, organizer of a monthly series called "Poetry Talk" at Africa House, and has recently begun offering writing consultation services to young professional women at www.beautyfullwriting.com.

www.ingramcontent.com/pod-product-compliance
Lightning Source LLC
LaVergne TN
LVHW041604070426
835507LV00011B/1308